Climb Inside

The INs and OUTs of
Using Jumbo Balloons on Stage

by Larry Moss

> **DISCLAIMER:** Climbing inside a 6 foot latex balloon can be dangerous. Following the advice provided here does not guarantee your safety. The author believes this to be the best advice for performing this stunt. It is still a stunt and you still may get hurt.
> ***Try this at your own risk.***

Copyright © 2007-2012 by Larry Moss
www.airigami.com

Photos by John Barthelmes
Duplication in whole or in part is prohibited without written permission from the author.

Second Edition

Contents

Acknowledgments 6
Why write this? 7
Can I learn to do it? 8
Is it safe? 9
Types of balloons 11
Preparing balloons for the stunt 12
Inflating the balloon 13
What to wear 15
Getting in 16
Reassurances 19
Keeping the balloon inflated 20
Getting out of the balloon 23
Routining 24
About the Author 29

Acknowledgments

Many people climbed inside balloons before me. The history of the stunt is a bit of a mystery. Quite a few people claim to have originated the idea. Thanks go out to all of the people that have done this in the past. Many paths lead to Skip Banks as the person that at least made the stunt popular, even if he wasn't the first entertainer to play with this. So thanks to Skip for his contributions.

The actress/burlesque dancer Sally Rand is regularly credited with creating the "bubble dance" circa 1934. From photos and video I've seen, and the little bit of information I've been able to read about her, I'm fairly certain she never entered the balloon. However, it does look like she was instrumental in making the first jumbo balloons and the first to use them on stage. Although I believe she never was inside the balloon, the photos certainly create the illusion that she was and she deserves thanks for starting this whole thing.

Thanks to Todd Neufeld for the time he put into editing this book and for trying to help sort out the history of climbing into balloons. Thanks to Lorinda Ferrell for working with me on finding and getting the right balloons, including playing with imprints so I could get just the right look for my show.

Why write this?

When I first learned of climbing inside a giant balloon, I was instantly interested in trying it. Unfortunately, finding information about it, even something as simple as buying the balloons, seemed to be a closely guarded secret by the few that found it before me. I'm all for protecting routines, but it was the stunt that I wanted to learn. I'm someone that has no interest in doing what others do from a performance standpoint. I knew that if I learned how to perform this, I would not do it the same way as other performers. It seemed odd that no one would share.

Time passed. I did learn the ins and outs of climbing in a balloon, mostly through experimentation. Very quickly, other balloon entertainers started asking me for information and help. At first, my gut instinct was to keep quiet, as those before me had done. It had been beaten into me by a few people that sharing this would somehow hurt those of us already doing it. That is, until I learned how many other people were trying it unsafely. It scared me to learn what people were trying. It made me sad to learn which balloons they were wasting money on, and the misunderstandings they had about the balloons themselves.

With that mindset I decided the best thing to do would be to compile my thoughts on the subject and, rather than hide secrets, teach it and encourage others to do it well. To those concerned or upset that I'm teaching this so openly, I can only encourage you to sit back and watch what someone new to this comes up with. I expect that all of us can learn something new or at least be entertained by new routines developed from an old stunt.

Can I learn to do it?

One of the things that makes this so interesting to the audience is that no one expects you to stretch a balloon open enough to squeeze into it. But let's face it, it's rubber. Rubber stretches. You do have to start with the right type of balloon - one with a wide neck. Outside of that, the actual mechanics of it are fairly easy.

That doesn't mean you'll get it on the first try. It does take practice and the first few times, you may find yourself a little worn out. With patience, just about anyone will be able to do it. If you're physically fit enough to last through a stage performance of another kind, you should be fine doing this. I've seen some fairly hefty performers work their way into the balloon. If your waist is too large for the neck of the balloon (I've never seen it, but it's certainly possible), it can be just as entertaining to an audience to make it partially into the balloon and get "stuck".

www.mrbirch.com

Is it safe?

As with anything you try, you should consider all safety issues first. This is not without its dangers. I emphatically give one piece of advice that will help ensure your safety:

> **DO NOT DO THIS WITHOUT ANOTHER PERSON PRESENT.**
> Even if everything goes wrong, someone else around with scissors will always be able to cut you out of the balloon.

The things we typically worry about with balloons are not a problem with giant balloons. Using the right balloon eliminates most of them. For example, it's not unusual to hear about minor eye injuries caused by a fragment of an exploded balloon hitting an eye while twisting balloon animals. The loud popping sound can also be painful if it occurs too close to someone's ear. With most of the 6 foot balloons sold today, this isn't a concern. The balloon is thick enough and heavy enough that the edges of a burst balloon travel too slowly to hurt you, even if it slaps against your body. There are some 6 foot balloons on the market that are extremely thin and feel almost like the usual small decorative and twisting balloons. However, ==avoiding balloons that are too thin and light is usually a good idea== for this stunt anyway since you want something durable enough to handle the abuse you're putting it through.

A common concern is the length of time you can stay inside the balloon. You can breathe normally inside the balloon for quite a while. After all, it's filled with air. To figure out just how much air let's look at a few numbers. Let's assume we want to leave a lot of room for our bodies and only inflate the balloon to a 5 foot diameter. That also gives us a lot of room for error. Assuming the balloon is perfectly round, a 5 foot balloon will contain 65 cubic feet or 1,840 liters of air. According to numbers published by the California Evironmental Protection Agency, an average male that has been exerting the energy required to run at 5 mph breathes about 58 liters of air per minute. That means that this theoretical male would have enough air inside the balloon for 31 minutes.

Of course, those numbers were selected conservatively. Inflating the balloon to its full six feet will get you substantially more air, and the energy exerted while doing the stunt should not be sufficient to match that of running at 5 mph. That was simply the category in the CEPA study that used the most air and therefore the most conservative for our calculations.

There are a few potential concerns about breathing inside the balloon. One is the powder found on the inside. This will be in any balloon, and getting any foreign particles in your lungs probably isn't ideal, but the amount of powder is fairly small compared to the amount of breathable air. If this is still a concern for you, feel free to turn the balloon inside out and wash off the excess powder prior to the performance.

Another concern is the balloon deflating around you if you don't close the neck well enough as you go in. This will reduce the amount of breathable air. This is probably the most dangerous situation that can occur with this stunt. There are two things that are absolute musts for doing this. As stated strongly above, **a partner nearby with scissors** will always be able to free you from the balloon long before you'd run out of air. The second suggestion is to **have scissors on your body as you climb inside.** No one in their right mind would do a fire act without a fire extinguisher and other safety equipment nearby. In this stunt, scissors are your fire extinguisher. I recommend two pairs of blunt tipped scissors. I keep one pair in a shirt pocket and one in a pants pocket. This way, no matter where you are in the process of entering the balloon, at least one pair of scissors is accessible to you. The reason for the blunt tip (and my reason for suggesting scissors over knives) is so you don't accidently stab yourself while contorting your body.

The last major concern I have for safety is that the space is sufficiently large for my performance. I use an opaque balloon, which means I can't see what's around me once I'm inside. It is very easy to lose your sense of direction as you bumble around on stage without the aid of your eyes. It is quite conceivable that you could fall off the edge of the stage or crash into and break things around you. **Make sure you have enough open space for the stunt.**

Types of balloons

This is not going to be a comprehensive review of all the giant balloons out there. I hate to mention a specific product because things change over time. What I name now as my favorite balloon may fall out of favor over time, or worse, become unavailable. But, providing information on how to perform the stunt and not name at least one balloon that can be used will leave many people stumped when it comes to actually trying this out. This is not an endorsement for a balloon. It's what works for me, right now, at the time of this writing.

I use Rifco 72-inch balloons. The most important part here isn't the size of the balloon, but the size of the neck. A lot of people getting started are tempted to buy larger balloons, thinking that will make things easier. That's an incorrect assumption. Many of the larger balloons, notably the chloroprene balloons on the market, have a narrower neck that can't be stretched open. The Rifco balloons also have a neck that's long enough that we can cut the nozzle off and still have a long enough neck to handle the balloon. Lastly, Rifco makes a strong, flexible balloon that can withstand a huge amount of abuse as I roll around the stage. Thinner balloons that I've tried just can't handle the abuse and burst prematurely.

There is one difficulty I've had with Rifco balloons that's easily correctable. I find that many of the balloons I receive are stiff and won't inflate easily. This can actually happen with any latex balloon, and I've seen it in several brands. It is not a problem unique to Rifco. For some reason however, the Rifcos seem to have this problem more often. The fix is to toss them in a clothes dryer on it's coolest setting for about 10-15 minutes. This works much better to restore the balloon to its soft form than to work it by stretching it. In fact, this works so well to soften the balloons, I highly recommend that **all balloons used for this be tossed in the dryer 24-48 hours prior to performing the stunt.**

Preparing balloons for the stunt

As mentioned earlier, it is highly recommended the balloons to be used for this stunt be tossed in a clothes dryer within 48 hours prior to your performance.

The lip of the balloon is thick enough that stretching it enough to get through is difficult. **Cutting the nozzle off the balloon makes the stunt much easier.** Be careful to cut only the lip and not the full neck. You want as much of the neck to be there as possible. The neck serves two purposes for us. It provides something to hold and it makes the balloon less likely to tear at the opening.

A 72 inch balloon made by Rifco. The thick lip is cut off, but the neck was left as long as possible.

An ordinary garden leaf blower is used to inflate the balloon

Inflating the balloon

Any air blower will work, but you're looking to push as much air as you can as quickly as possible. Currently, I use a **starndard electric leaf blower.** There are a variety of choices in this area from compact ones that are easy to throw in a suitacse for travel, to heftier ones that will inflate the balloons faster. Some of the smaller ones are cordless and use rechargeable batteries. Some performers find them easier to wield on stage.

Do not use a leaf blower that's also a vacuum/mulcher if it's been used for outdoor work. You don't want to take the chance of blowing fragments of leaves, sticks or other things that have passed through it into the air you're going to breathe. You also don't want those objects to be in there rubbing against, and weakening, the balloon.

If you plan on inflating the balloon on stage, you may want to consider the audible volume of the device you use. I use an AC powered leaf blower that inflates my balloons in about 30 seconds. I happen to like the look of a big orange, outdoor extension cord running across my stage, and the volume just adds drama to the whole thing. **I do make sure my microphone is turned off before I turn on the blower.**

Don't over-inflate the balloon. Remember to leave space for yourself inside the balloon. You can judge the size of the balloon by your own height. Unless you're particularly short, don't plan on standing upright inside the balloon and don't try to climb into it when it's inflated to a height greater than your own. I like to inflate the balloon to slightly greater than my height and then let out enough air that the top of the balloon is level with my eyes.

Note that even though they are called "round" balloons, they aren't completely spherical. They're made on flat forms. This means that you'll be able to see what looks like a seam along the circumference of the balloon. The balloon will inflate to a greater diameter along this "seam" than along any other axis. A balloon marketed as having a 72 inch diameter may only be 72 inches on the axis marked by this seam. Always inflate the balloon in the same orientation so that you can quickly judge the size. I inflate the balloon so this seam runs parallel to my body.

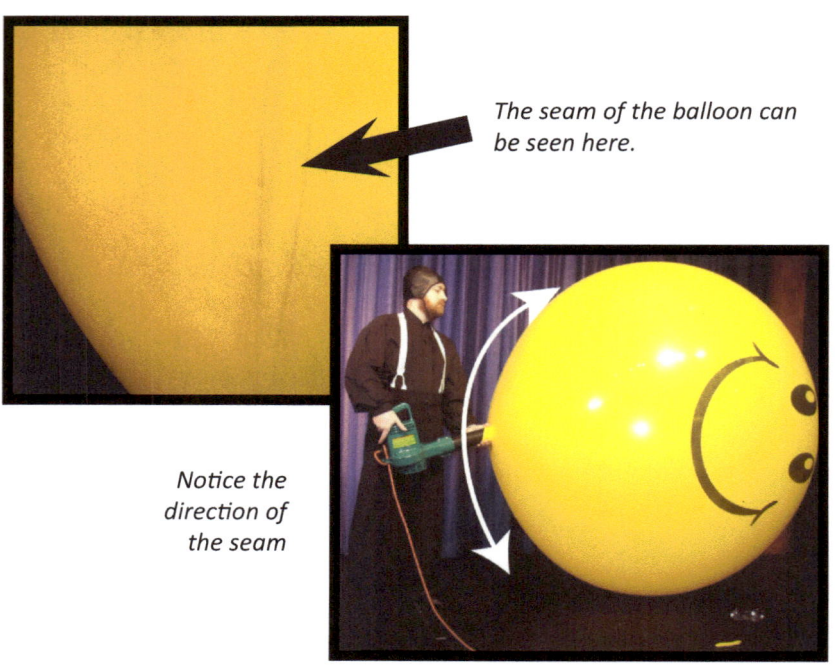

The seam of the balloon can be seen here.

Notice the direction of the seam

What to wear

Clothing should not be ignored or left entirely until you start building your routine. The clothing you wear can play a part in how easy or hard it is to do this stunt, so even for practice there is appropriate dress. You want maximum flexibility and maneuverability inside the balloon. You want to ==avoid clothing that's rough.== Jeans are particularly hard to work in due to the stiffness and roughness of the material and the rivets typically found around the pockets. It's easy to get a balloon caught up on the rivets as you slide the balloon past your waist.

Tight fitting clothing may seem like the way to go, but unless you have the body for it and you plan on wearing that on stage, that's not the best idea for learning. You can still do this with loose fitting clothes. The smoothness of the material will have a greater impact on the difficulty than how close it is to your body. In fact, when you get to choosing the right clothing for the performance, you may want clothing that's extremely loose fitting that will hide any awkwardness you demonstrate while climbing in the balloon.

While I've seen it done, ==I would not recommend doing this with much bare skin.== The balloon will be rubbing against your body, grabbing skin and hair as you pull various body parts through. Wearing long sleeves can make the process a lot less painful.

If you have long hair, you'll want to find a way to cover it to prevent it getting caught and pulling as the balloon goes over your head. This can take some creative routining to make it all make sense. A tight fitting hat or swim cap can solve this problem.

While I've never found eye protection to be necessary, goggles can add a bit of humor to the whole thing.

Getting in

I don't think it can be stated too many times: you should never do this alone. When learning, aside from adding safety to the stunt, you can sometimes use the assitance of someone watching to tell you where you're getting caught up on the balloon. The other person can also lend a hand in stretching the balloon at particularly troubling points.

With the balloon inflated, insert one arm into the neck. You can stop at any thicker part of your arm since your arm will act as a seal to block the air from escaping.

Insert your arm up to the shoulder.

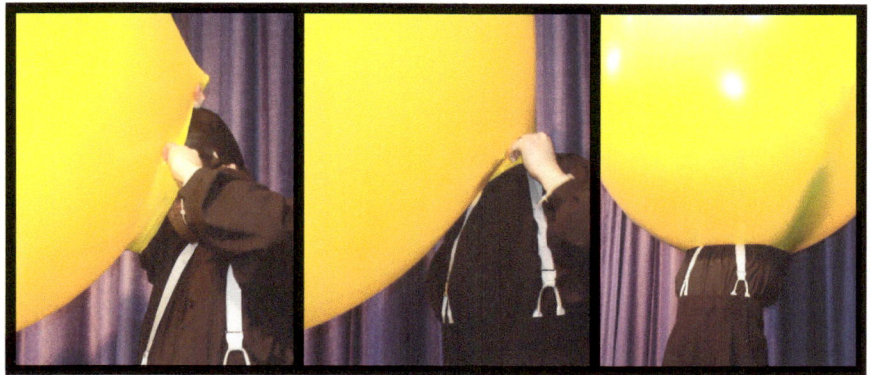

With your second hand, in one motion, stretch the neck of the balloon open and pull it over your head. Without stopping, continue to insert your second arm.

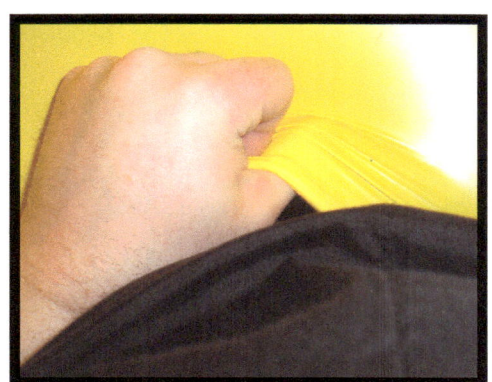

From the inside, work it down your body by stretching the neck a little with your hands and pushing it downward.

Keep that up until the balloon reaches your waist and stop.

This is the view inside the balloon.

Don't push it past your hips until you're ready to push it the rest of the way down, or at least pull one leg all the way in. If you push it partially down both legs you'll lose air from the space between your legs. *No matter how hard you try, you can't bring your legs close enough together to stop air from leaking out.*

Pull one leg all the way into the balloon. Now sitting or laying on the floor, you can pull the second leg all the way in. That's it. You've done it. From inside, stick a hand out and wave the crowd. Stick your head out and smile.

Reassurances

Balloons pop. If they didn't, this wouldn't be nearly as interesting a stunt for the audience. When you're practicing, expect to break a few balloons. You'll get better. Still, no matter how much you practice, some balloons will break in performance. Always have a spare around for those times.

When a balloon pops during practice, look at how it broke. Often you can see where the tear started and get hints as to the cause. Common causes are dirty floors, belt buckles, and clothing made from rough fabrics. Harder to see are small rips in the neck from stretching it too roughly. If the tear is happening close to the neck, make sure you haven't cut off too much of it when preparing the balloon. Make sure you also haven't over-inflated the balloon.

Notes:

Keeping the balloon inflated

Once you've gotten inside the balloon, you'll want to spend a little time in there to give the audience a chance to see what you've done. Maybe you want to do a little more while in there. In any event, air rushing out too quickly will shorten your performance, cut down on the time you can breathe, and otherwise be quite uncomfortable.

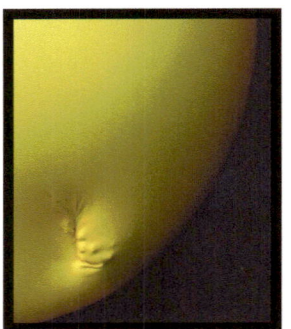

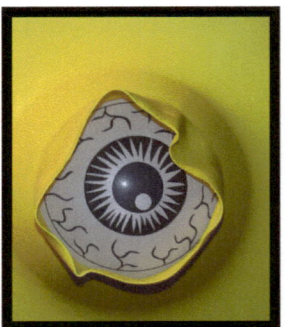

A fist grabbing the balloon tightly

Plugging the hole with a balloon from the inside...

...this is what's seen on the outside.

The most obvious way to stop the air from escaping is the same way you did it on the way in. Put an arm, leg, or head into the neck of the balloon again. You can also inflate a small round balloon to stick in the open neck in the same way you would a body part. Another option is to grab the neck of the balloon and hold it from the inside, closing it off.

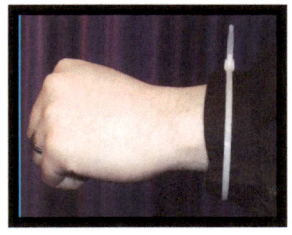

If you want to free up both of your hands so you can do something else while in the balloon, **the neck can be sealed with a zip tie.** You can do this by wrapping a long zip tie loosely around your wrist so it can still be pulled off, over your hand.

While inside the balloon, hold the neck of the balloon with the hand wearing the zip tie and slide it from your wrist to the balloon. Now pull it tight.

If all else fails and you just can't keep as much air in the balloon as you'd like, it's always possible to have your assistant re-inflate the balloon. Once you're inside the balloon, you're probably going to move around and reposition yourself, freeing up the neck for the blower to be inserted from the outside.

Slide the zip tie over your hand and pull it tight to seal

The cinched up balloon, from the inside...

The cinched up balloon, from the outside.

Getting out of the balloon

Getting out is much easier than getting in. If you're fully inside the balloon, just pop it. It's fast and dramatic. The question from most people just starting this is, "but can I re-use a balloon to save money?" It's true that the balloons are expensive, but I do not recommend you try to save them. At least not to repeat the same stunt. **Once you've stretched and abused the balloon, the chances of them popping the next time around are much greater.** If the timing and appearance of your show depends on this working, you don't want to hurt your chances of success.

If you really do want to save the balloon, you can get out following the same steps as you did going in. Consider though, in addition to the chance of damaging the balloon too much to use again anyway, you've already built to the high point of the routine. You want to end with a "bang". You want the dramatic ending. Once the audience has watched you climb in, they don't really need to sit through you repeating the process to get out.

Assuming you've followed my advice and have scissors on you, popping the balloon won't be a problem. But what if you ignored my advice? I learned the hard way when I was getting started that you sometimes have **sharp objects hidden on your clothing that you can use in those emergency situations.** I was doing a library show, was ready to get out, and discovered my scissors were missing. I tried clawing my way out. I tried biting my way out. I was bouncing around in the balloon as much as I could, hoping it would burst. I even called out for help. All that happened was increased laughter from my audience who thought all of this was intentional. Then I realized that I could pull my belt off and use the pin on the buckle to puncture and tear the balloon.

Routining

Once you've done the work and learned how to get in, the next step is building the routine. As I stated earlier, my purpose here is not to present you with a full routine. I want to help you get started safely and easily. The rest of the work is up to you. I will, however, give some ideas to consider as starting points.

Let's look at it from the very beginning. **You don't have to inflate the balloon in front of the audience**. You can pre-inflate the balloon and close it with a zip tie or binder clip that can easily be removed when you want it. This will save a little time on stage and protect the audience from the noise of the blower. If this is being done for live TV or anywhere timing is critical, even if you normally inflate the balloon in front of the audience, you might want to **have another backstage that's already inflated in case the first one pops**. This will keep the show moving along.

If you choose to inflate the balloon in front of the audience, keep in mind that **your blower will probably make a huge amount of noise.** Don't attempt to speak over it and don't count on any background music being audible. If you've got one of the quieter blowers (which are still loud) and you're in a large enough venue, it may not be all that loud to the audience, so music coming through an amplifier may mask out some of the inflation noise. But don't assume that will be the case in too many performance areas.

The color of the balloon you use can say a lot. One of the first choices you'll have to make is whether to use a clear or opaque balloon. There are advantages to each. A clear balloon will allow you to do something inside the balloon that the audience can see. You can dance. You can do an underwater routine with fish swimming around you. Opaque balloons will allow you to do things that are completely hidden from the audience. You can then surprise them with something new when you come out.

If you choose opaque balloons, **pick a color that works with your costuming and set** and go with it. In a way, this will be a costume. The appearance of the balloon should match your character.

You need to decide what this should look like to your audience. Are you after a scary or a comical look? Is your body really creating the effect you want? I've had some people tell me that it looks like the balloon is eating me. You can play with the man-eating balloon idea, or as I prefer, pretend you just got stuck and you're trying to get out.

Do you want to talk to the audience while you're inside? If so, wear a mic so you're heard clearly. The balloon will not interfere with a wireless microphone that needs to transmit a signal to the outside. However, you do need to **make sure that the mic you are wearing won't get in your way or get caught as you climb in.** Also make sure your mic and body pack can handle the abuse you're going to put it through while doing a very physical stunt.

The material on the following 2 pages is normally provided with a 5 inch smiley balloon to audience volunteers, potential clients, and others. Make something similar for your own act.

Build Your Own Larry Moss!

For years, audience members have been asking if they could take Larry home with them after his shows. The answer has always been the same. There just isn't enough of him to go around.

The solution is finally here: with this Build Your Own Larry kit, you can have your very own favorite balloon entertainer in your home. Never forget the fun time you had at his performance when you have your own model of Larry inside his 6 foot man-eating balloon.

DIRECTIONS:

1. Cut along dotted lines to remove shoes from instruction sheet. Make sure to also cut the circle between the two shoes.
3. Inflate smiley balloon to approximately 5 inches in diameter. Tie balloon.
4. Insert nozzle of smiley balloon into hole between shoes.
5. Enjoy!

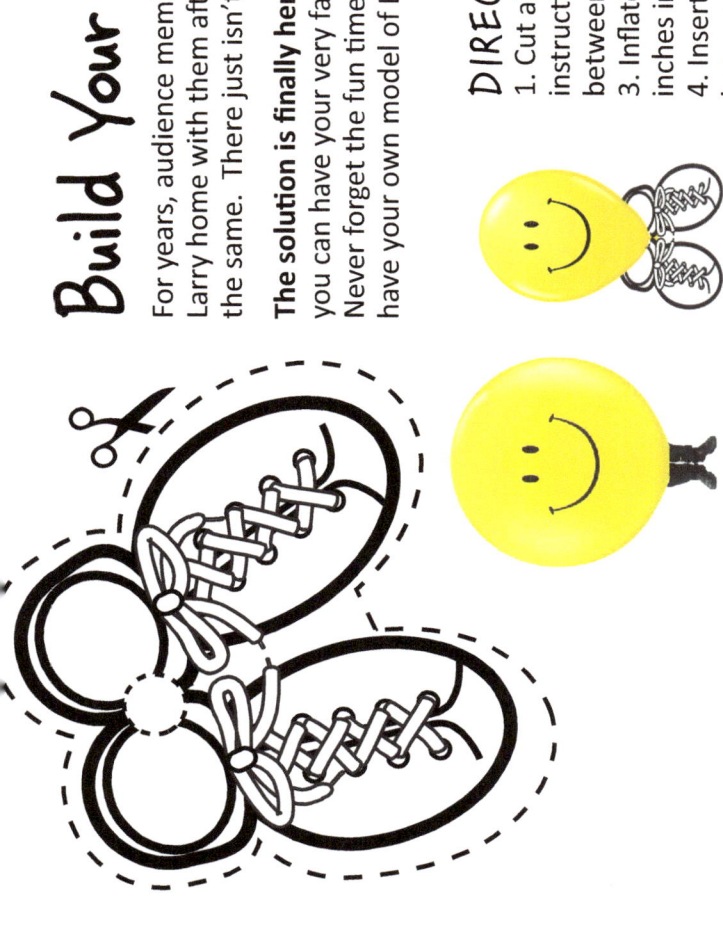

Larry in the balloon   Completed kit

For more fun, visit: **www.airigami.com**

STAGE SHOWS

How to Catch a Mouse: Simple Machines at Work

Balloons are used in this one-man show to construct a Rube Goldberg-style mousetrap intended to solve the problem of a mouse on the loose. Many student volunteers are used to aid in the construction of this working machine.

www.howtocatchamouse.com

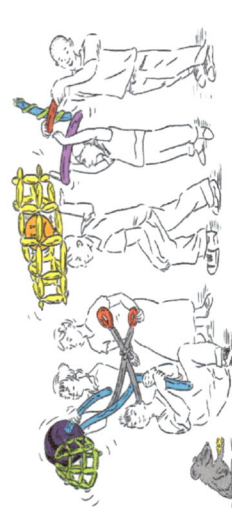

Magic, Danger, Suspense, and Silliness

In this two-man show, comedy, magic, balloons, juggling, and "danger" are combined in an unusual fashion, leaving family audiences amused and amazed. This show is the result of two people ignoring the warnings and "trying this at home."

www.wearesolo.com

AND MORE...

Strolling Entertainment

Have Larry at your event twisting unusual balloon creations for all your guests. Animals, hats, costumes, and even portraits of you and your friends.

Custom Balloon Creations

Have Larry design a sculpture just for you. Anything from a few balloons to a few thousand balloons is possible to make your event stand out. **www.airigami.com**

Airigami • 1115 E Main St • Rochester, NY 14609 • (585) 359-8695

About the Author

Vincent van Gogh used paint. Auguste Rodin worked in bronze. Larry Moss shapes air with the use of balloons. Larry's unusual art has been displayed in 12 countries on four continents. His achievements have been recognized by the Guinness Book of World Records, Smithsonian Magazine, Cabinet, American Profile, Ripley's Believe It or Not!, CNN and PBS.

Larry's accomplishments include setting the world's record for the largest non-round balloon sculpture, using more than 40,000 balloons to construct two 40-foot tall soccer players. He also built the first and only piloted latex balloon sculpture, as well as Balloon Manor, the 10,000-square-foot haunted houses made entirely out of balloons.

Renowned in his field for these large and technically challenging sculptures, Larry is also an experienced teacher of his art, as well as the author of several ballooning books.

Larry has a degree in applied math and computer science, as well as a master's in elementary education. His unusual career combines his loves of teaching, entertaining and science, and he's performed for audiences all over the world – from street corners and schools to rock concerts and television.

For more information about Larry, visit: **airigami.com.**